FROM *POISON* TO MEDICINE

Be Blessed

Michael Stanley

My grandmother, mother, and aunt.
Who stood in the gap, and never gave up on me.

FROM *POISON* TO MEDICINE

Michael W. Stanley

From Poison to Medicine ISBN: 979-8-9859098-0-7

Printed in the United States of America 2022 - First
Edition

Cover photo: Mr. McKinley White, Moving in Motion by
Mac
Cover Design: Ms. Melanie West, Kingdom Kreations
Editing: Ms. Veronica G. Ferrell

Unless otherwise indicated, Scriptures quoted are from the
King James Version (KJV), New International Version
(NIV), and the English Standard Version (ESV). All rights
reserved.

The Gift of A Son

No one can count on the future or know what they
someday might do.

But if I could have chosen the son that I wanted the one
I'd have picked would be you.

I'd have wished for your great sense of humor and
dreamed of your spirit and style

I'd have hoped for your love and affection imagined
the joy in your smile…

Life holds some gifts and surprises and one of the best
there could be is having a son whose exactly been
given to me.

-Momma

This book is dedicated to my dear Mother
Ms. Pauline Brown

MOTHER

My dear Mother was always there for me. She stood with me and encouraged me throughout some of the worst times of my life. My mother was there no matter what! She was the glue that kept our family close. She was the best part of my life. I could never ask for a better life than the one my dear mother created for me. I love and miss my dear Mother very much, but I carry her with me in my heart each day. I thank God for allowing me to have a strong, praying, loving, and supporting Mother.

Thank you

I would like to thank God for his grace, his love, and for allowing me to live again to experience the freedom to move, breathe and to love. I also thank God for giving me the opportunity to tell my story!

I would like to extend a special and heartfelt thanks to my dear friend, Dr. Saphonia Michelle Butler. She has been my biggest cheerleader. Dr. Butler has been a prime source for pushing and encouraging me to do what God has called me to do. She wore the hat of photographer, is responsible for some of the photos that I included in my book, and she also assisted in making decisions for my book cover. Last, but not least, she assisted me in finishing one of many projects this book!

To my friend, Evangelist Veronica G. Ferrell for also continuing to encourage me, and for her professional and skilled talent in editing and proof-reading my book. I also thank her for her assistance during this process.

Ms. Gale Saccarelli, Esq. thank you for representing me during such a difficult time and process in my life, and for writing the forward of this book.

Apostle Stanley, Dr. Shiral, and Pastor-Elect Stephany

Smith, thank you for believing in me, encouraging me, allowing God to use you to speak into my life, and for allowing me to be used in your ministry.

Special thanks to Ms. Melanie D. West, Kingdom Kreations, for her support and assistance in creating my book cover.

Special thanks to Mr. McKinley White, Moving in Motion by Mac, for being my photographer for my book cover. Finally, I would like to thank my family, especially my four brothers, who have been there with me throughout all my pain and has put up with my mess over the years!

And to everyone who will read these pages.

TABLE OF CONTENTS

Forward - 12

Introduction - 14

My Reality- 17

My Seed - 24

A Hero? Really? - 26

Authority - 29

Where It All Started - 32

The Lifestyle - 38

Power - 42

My Journey To Redemption - 51

The Poison Within - 54

Being Incarcerated - 60

Super Max -63

Disciplinary and Solitary Confinement - 65

God Brought Me Thorough - 71

Sex and Homosexuality in the Prison - 74

TABLE OF CONTENTS

College - 79

Transformation - 83

Sanctification - 94

Back in the Courtroom - 96

I am Free! Thank God! I am Free! - 98

Back in Society/Recidivism - 102

Poverty - 107

Fear - 111

Seeing God - 115

Rejection Faulty Beliefs - 117

Helping Others - 119

Forgiveness - 121

My Recent Encounter with God - 124

Growing and Moving Forward - 128

Things to Ponder -132

About the Book - 135

About the Author - 138

FORWARD

I met Mr. Michael Stanley for the first time in the mid 1990's. I was a career Public Defender in the Prince George's County, Maryland, a suburb of Washington, D.C. At the time Mr. Stanley was serving a life sentence for a drug related homicide conviction. I was not the original attorney for his case. I was assigned the case in 1995 to see if there was any type of post-conviction relief still available to him.

In 1986 Mr. Stanley had pleaded not guilty but had gone to trial and had been convicted of First-Degree Murder. By 1995 he had already exhausted all traditional forms of the judicial relief such as appeals, motions for modification of sentence, etc. All efforts to reduce his sentence had been denied. However, Mr. Stanley had a few things in his favor. He had an impressive prison record for most of his years of incarceration. He earned a college degree, and he started the first counseling program in prison. He had a dedicated and persistent mother who was willing to do whatever it took to save her son. Because of Mr. Stanley's accomplishments and the many accolades from the prison staff, teachers, and clergy, I was able to convince the County Prosecutor's office not to oppose Mr. Stanley's request for a reduced sentence. Without opposition from the State, the Judge granted his request! Mr. Stanley was released from prison in 2004!

Since his release, Mr. Michael Stanley, has worked hard to rebuild his life. Mr. Stanley has used his experience, education, and influence to make positive changes in his community. Mr. Stanley mentors' young people and provides guidance to individuals struggling with re-entry issues, behavior issues, and counsels those with addiction problems. For the last seventeen years, Mr. Michael Stanley has used his intellect, his experiences, his education, and his compassion to make meaningful contributions to the world around him!

Gale Saccarelli, Esq.

INTRODUCTION

Sin is a *poison* which must be eradicated at any cost. A man must make the necessary commitment to find victory over sin. One must understand the realm where this great struggle must take place.

One Friday evening, as I stood in a county court room awaiting sentencing, I found myself in what appeared to be a deep sleep; a coma, for quite some time, at least I thought so. Only to wake up to face the reality, that I had just got sentence to life plus 20 years with no parole. My beginnings, I thought just became my end!

After having a long and weary day in the court room. The Judge didn't make it any better. He started saying a lot of disparaging things about me. The Judge stated before the court, that I was a menace to society. The Judge also stated that as long as he was positioned on the bench, I would never, ever, see freedom again! He also had the nerve to call me an animal and made other degrading remarks to me as well. In that very moment, my life truly flashed before me! Reality hit me, and it hit hard! I was going to spend the rest of my life in Prison! I was one to always believe that if you did the crime, you would have to face any punishment that was granted, but I didn't think that I would get caught.

Reality hit me! I was literally given a death sentence! But, in my mind, I was trying to figure out how I was going to get out of this situation! I was determined that I was going to do something about it!

The wonderful end to my story is that I found God, and God restored me to normalcy. Better yet, He restored my innocence and I still have a sound mind and can remember what happened! God has given me the pure and sensitive spirit of a person that has ranged from knowing corruption to being transformed from the inside out and to a person that value and respect the lives of others.

My Life Changing Experiences
I thank God for answering my prayers!
I thank God for delivering me!
I thank God that He put mercy in the heart of an Attorney that helped me get through the judiciary process; as well as, given mercy in the heart of the Judge.

The same Judge that I saw that day, who spoke negative words over my life, was the same Judge, who I saw many years later, in the court room that released me back into society!

Michael W. Stanley

If the Son therefore shall make you free, ye shall be free indeed. **John 8:36**

MY REALITY

Although the reality of life can be tough to handle at times, it is where the good things in life also reside. One must experience the consequences of his actions in the real world.

I had little respect for reality. My life had just started, as I was entering adulthood. I continued to allow my *poisoned* mind to make poor choices, and I avoided the consequences of my bad behavior. Finally, I woke up and realized that I had forfeited my life! My thoughts were all over the place, and I was trying to understand, how in the world had I become a victim? I became a by-product of my environment, where my role models were drug dealers, pimps, and everything else that came with that lifestyle?

I recently had a milestone birthday, and Lord knows that I didn't think I was going to make it to see that day. I am the middle child, out of five boys. There was no father figure around to help shape and mold us from a man's perspective. Therefore, my dear mother raised all of us by herself, with no monetary support from any of our fathers; therefore, we were raised on welfare.

My dear mother worked hard for many years. She

finally managed to get a job working for the Department of Labor, which allowed us to eventually move out of the projects. Her original intent was to move out of the projects. She never wanted us to stay in the projects. But we stayed there long enough that the **poison** from the projects had already seeped into our young minds. I was already fascinated with what I saw on the streets and all it entailed. I watched the pimps, drug dealers, prostitutes, bank robbers, stickup boys and the men that were living the fine life in the streets.

I remember one day. It was the first day of school, and my dear mother was walking me and my two younger brothers to school. As we were walking, I saw drug dealers who wore very nice clothes and jewelry that drove fancy cars. You must understand that pimps, prostitutes, and drug dealers were all we saw around daily. But this day, I couldn't take my eyes off what I saw. I found it fascinating, and I wanted to be a part of it. I knew then that this is what I would be! My dear mother literately had to yank me by my arm, because my attention was drawn to what I saw on the streets that day. I constantly kept looking back as we were walking, I couldn't take my eyes away from what I saw! My dear mother told me then, that if I did not focus on getting an education that I would end up like what I saw on the streets. She referred to them as "bums".

Living in the projects was all I knew, and it was fun to me, because there was always something exciting going on. There were parties, street gambling, people fighting, boys playing sports, and other families cooking out during the summer months. It was not anything you didn't see, because people did everything! They did not hide anything! We were young boys living the fast life. This was our reality and all that we knew.

My dear mother made it her business to involve us in sports and any after school activities to help keep us off the streets. My brothers and I were all involved in sports in school, as well as, in many sports/recreational activities at the Boys Club. We all excelled in all sports, to include boxing. We had close to approximately 300 trophies between the five of us. We were all well known for our achievements throughout our neighborhood. Therefore, to us, we had a wonderful, normal life. As a result, any positive advice that my dear mother gave us, went in one ear and out the other. I also remember, one day, I told my hard-working dear mother that I am going to make more money than she could ever make by selling drugs. What a foolish thing to say!

It is written in the Bible, that words carry power, and the words that we speak can either offer life or death! Anything negative that is spoken can become death to you or any situation in your life! As I think back on it now, being at a very young age, and very immature, my statement was made from stupidity, but that is what I had on my mind at the time. My mind was already **poisoned**, and I preceded to start to live a destructive lifestyle.

The tongue has the power of life and death, and those who love it will eat its fruit. **Proverbs 18:21**

I got involved with criminal activities starting at the age of 13, in the streets of Washington, D.C. I started making bad choices and doing bad things, such as, hanging out late and hanging with the wrong crowd. I smoked weed, and constantly fought in school. I also started breaking into and stealing cars. I was also part of a neighborhood gang. What I realized today was that I had become a by-product of my environment, and I was sucked into the concept that the streets were the best way out of poverty, and education didn't matter. Boy was I wrong! Not to mention, my dear mother was an advocate when it came to education and wanted all her sons to pursue an education as a step toward making better choices in life.

In the area where we lived, we had many neighborhood gangs. Therefore, depending on where you lived, is what gang you were a part of. An example of that is, if you lived on M Street they had a gang, and if you lived on N Street, they had a gang and so forth. The gangs always included about 4 to 5 young men. My gang consisted of a group of 5 of us from the neighborhood. I was what we called back than the "front runner," and "the leader" of my gang. They listened to everything I told them to do and whatever I did, they just followed suit. I was the one that gave the orders and they carried out my orders, because they respected me. We were all determined young men and felt that nothing was going to stop us or get in the way of us doing whatever we wanted to do! We thought we were gangsters, and we really didn't know the meaning of such a word. All we knew is that we were bad boys, and we wanted to be gangsters.

My gang and I would hang out at each other's houses to watch gangster movies, movies about pimps; the more we watched the movies, we admired and wanted to be like the gangsters we saw on the streets of New York City. Therefore, we studied that type of behavior and lifestyle. We thought being a gangster was cool, and in my gang, we vowed that people were going to respect us and look up to us, bad boys! I really wanted to be that guy, the gangster that I saw in the movies. I wanted it so bad that I could taste it. Again, my mind was *poisoned* by what I saw and wanted to be!

My destructive life started between the ages of 13-17. At the age of 13 years old, I started smoking marijuana (weed) and having sex. My first encounter with the law was at the age of 15. I was arrested multiple times for stealing cars; therefore, I was given the youth act, which meant that I had to do a minimum of 18 months in a Juvenile Detention Center. There were several detention centers, in the Washington, D.C. metropolitan area, and I was assigned to go to Oak Hill Juvenile Detention Center.

Oak Hill Juvenile Detention Center was the district's maximum security juvenile detention facility, nevertheless all the facilities in the Washington, D.C. metropolitan area were overcrowded, decrepit and vermin-infested, ravaged by social ills and mired in fiscal dysfunction. In some cases, after you served your time given, you would be released back to your families. There were times also that if you were at the age of 18, you were waived to adult court, which meant that you would be charged as an adult, and then you would go straight to the Penitentiary.

Some young men around my age, for whatever reason, had anger problems. As for me, I had no excuse and nothing to blame for my behavior as a young kid. While growing up, I really didn't have any anger problems at all! Therefore, although I could get angry at times, I couldn't blame my behavior on being angry. I was a determined fearless young kid. I just loved the streets, and the streets loved me! The streets were my life, my bread and butter, and it was fun to me! Foolish stinking thinking! But you pay the price to be the so-called Boss!

For as he thinketh in his heart, so is he: **Proverbs 23:7**

I graduated from High School

MY SEED

Despite all the things that I was doing in the streets, there were also girls, girls, and more girls. Therefore, sex was also a part of my life, and I had no problem with being with any girl. I had an inviting personality, and I could get any girl to do what I wanted them to do.

Sleeping around and having unprotected sex, time and time again! I never thought nothing about it because it came with that type of lifestyle. Therefore, at the young age of 17, I was told that I was going to be a father. What!? Me!? I was a child myself. I had no idea of how to be a father. I certainly didn't want to become a father at that age!

My focus was still living the fast street life. I never slowed down and I didn't think much on being a part of anyone's life! Fatherhood? Nope!

All in all, and it took a little time, for me to learn to accept the fact that I had a child coming into this world. Eventually I wanted desperately to become a part of my child's life, but I had no idea how to be a father. I didn't know anything about having a relationship with anyone nor how to bond with an individual.

Two years later I was sent into the Penitentiary, and I could not have any contact with my child for many years. Eventually, as she got older, and with the help of my dear mother, my child was able to come see me. I knew that I had to learn how to bond with my child. I just remember that the times that I was able to see my child was always the highlight of my day. I always cherished being able to see and spend time with my darling child whom I loved very much! Today, I love and cherish her even more. I am very proud of my daughter!

A cherished moment and accomplishment with my daughter.

A HERO? REALLY?

My first encounter with the law, made me feel like a man. That was my introduction to the game, and it validated who I was. There were times when I came back home from the Juvenile Detention Center, for some apparent reason, I always got patted on the back by other young male kids. Young adult-men thought that if you spent any time in a Juvenile Detention Center, it was cool. The reality is that some young male kids, were afraid of doing the things that I was doing on the streets or afraid that they would get caught in some of the crimes that they were committing. Therefore, at some point in their lives they would slow down or even stop. There were also a few young males that tried to do the right thing, as it related to listening to their parents' advice. As for me, I usually chose the negative, destructive side of life. My buddies were always happy to see me return to my neighborhood after being in Juvenile Detention.

You must understand that I grew up in an environment where almost every young male was involved in a gang, and we all were involved in crimes throughout the neighborhood. When we got caught, we all, at some point, went to a youth detention center, and that was normal for us. No matter how little or how much time that you spent in a youth detention center, other young males would look up to you, as if you were a hero. In our environment corruption was easy to get into. Many of the young males' mind were already **poisoned**, including mine! In my mind, I was even more powerful, and my buddies thought I was tough, and they respected me even more after I got home! In their minds, I went somewhere that they had never been before. They looked up to me because, maybe, they hadn't gotten caught! I was on my way to hell, and I couldn't even see it. Can you believe that the "**poison**" can have your mind so brain-washed, that it places a seed in your mind that implants ideas like, "You are a Hero" just because you spent time in a Juvenile Detention facility!? Really!? How impractical! How naïve!!

When I spent time in the Juvenile Detention Center, the only thing that was on my mind was, doing some of the things that I did before and didn't get caught. How could I continue, to steal, sell drugs, and live such a destructive lifestyle and not get locked up again? I really thought that I could out smart everyone including the rules and regulations that were established for the society.

As time went on, there was an older man that took me under his wing. He told me that he was going to show me how to make money, as well as, get all the girls. It was music to my ears, so I started working for him. One of my first assignments was to hold the stash. I held large sums of money in a bag, and I loved it! I eventually went out on my own, because I wanted to make the large sums of money that I held for myself. Somewhere in the process I also learned that I loved playing with guns. Drugs, money and guns, goes hand in hand. When I put a gun in my hands, I thought that I was unstoppable, that nothing could stop me! I lost my mind thinking such a thing!

Therefore, I eventually became a stickup boy. I robbed everything and everybody. I used to comb the streets of Washington, D.C. looking for drug dealers and squealers! I wasn't as smart as I thought, because at some point, I was going to get caught, and I did. This started the beginning of a destructive lifestyle of being in and out of Juvenile Detention to Prison. I was living the big life, with my big stubborn headed self! A life of no fear at all!

AUTHORITY

I remember when I was 17 years old, I came home again after being locked up, in Juvenile Detention. Like I stated previously after I came back to my neighborhood, I literally had people patting me on my back looking up to me, making me feel special, like a hero, and I was eating it all up! I felt good about it! My mind was *poisoned* by the streets! I felt that nothing was going to keep me from doing what I wanted to do, I felt big and bad!

I hated the police and viewed authority as an obstruction, as the enemy, that was in the way. I regarded them as a nuisance; therefore, I kept doing whatever I wanted to do. I felt that I could run or talk my way out of any and everything. Since I was involved in criminal activity and making bad choices; I felt that anyone that was doing anything right, and being respectful, I viewed them as the enemy. Of course, any authority around was around for a reason, to bring discipline and add some structure into my life. But I didn't see anything positive about them at the time. I did not fear any authority. I was really blinded by the *poison* of the streets, and I honestly didn't care at all!

Therefore, between the ages of 15-17, I had been constantly in and out of Juvenile Detention. My dear mother couldn't do anything with me. She also tried to send me away to stay with other family members, thinking that a change from my environment would help, but that didn't work either. I still smoked weed and would find a girl in the neighborhood to have sex with. I constantly gave my extended family members a hard time as well, until they eventually got tired of dealing with me, and sent me back home. No one could handle my destructive behavior, and no one wanted to! I eventually got caught in all my mess, I got locked up and charged. This time I had to spend more time locked up than before. Eventually I was given probation, and by that time I felt that I was unstoppable and untouchable! I knew that the other young males that were a part of gangs and on the streets, were going to look up to me even more, and respect me without a doubt! With any mention of my name, people were going to know not to cross me! Anyway, if you had the nerve to cross me, you were subject to get hurt!

Michael W. Stanley

The neighborhood today

WHERE IT ALL STARTED

I was born and raised in Washington, D.C. by my dear mother, in a single-family household. I am the 3rd born, or you could say, the middle child, of 5 boys. Therefore, some of my personality traits reflected that, I was the mediator, an avoider of conflict, a problem solver, the one that had many friends, was extremely loyal to peer groups, and independent. I was a "Maverick", which means, shiny, bright, and brilliant. Although perfectionism can be found in any birth order, it is normally dominant in almost all "first born" and "only child" children. But that wasn't the case for me. I am the 3rd born, yet I also am a perfectionist too!

When a person's trait is a perfectionist. They are usually very difficult, and nit-picky, which can often be very subtle. Therefore, any little thing can drive the perfectionists crazy, because nothing ever seems to be good enough to them unless things are done by them. Perfectionists can be very hard on themselves, which makes it easy for them to be hard on others. Therefore, I can be very difficult at times. A middle child can also go in any direction. It depends on how they branch off from the older brother or sister in the informative years. Therefore, with my traits, and because of the *poison* in my mind, it was easy for me to fit into the destructive lifestyle that I chose.

My older brother was someone that I looked up to, and he was my only role model. My brother had a heart of a protector and he protected me and my other brothers. He was like our bodyguard, and out of people respecting him, it made our lives a little bit easier on the streets. My brother was also a drug dealer who hung out in the streets as well. I thought he was a cool dude, therefore, I wanted to be cool too! He eluded the law for quite sometime until he finally got caught. But he never did a substantial amount of time in and out of jail like I did. Those experiences taught my brother some lessons, therefore he stopped being in the game.

At a very young age, I was given the nickname "Sweet Tooth," because, I ate a lot of candy. I was also known on the streets by that nickname. What I didn't realize at the time, that having such a nickname, would eventually be a problem for me while incarcerated.

Michael W. Stanley

This is where 5 boys lived with their dear mother in the projects of Washington, D.C.

This is where it all started, living the life of destruction

As mentioned previously, I traveled in a different circle, as a young male on the streets. I had a man (older mentor) to take me under his wing and show me the ropes of the street life. Therefore, eventually, the crowd I hung out with was around my age or much younger. I eventually became a different type of leader on the streets than my older brother. I had been in and out of Juvenile Detention as a teenager. Furthermore, I gave my dear mother the most problems out of any one of my other brothers.

Throughout the years, Juvenile Detention and Prison, had shaped and molded me; it basically, taught me how to be a tough man. Although my dear mother did her best, she still could not teach me or my brothers how to be men.

The streets taught us, we had to learn or figure it out ourselves, because our fathers, nor a positive father figure was around. Therefore, as I previously stated, I was influenced by drug dealers, pimps, and back stabbers. All bad guys!

Out of my own personal experiences and bad choices, I became a certain type of man. The way I feel is different from any of my brothers. My past lifestyle, and the school of "hard knocks" shaped and molded me into a new type of man – "a man different than I was in the past, a better man for today's society."

My brothers and I participated in many recreational activities at this location

THE LIFESTYLE

My dear mother, in my opinion, did a wonderful job in raising us on her own. In our eyes, we didn't know what being poor was, although we lived in a poor environment. My dear mother always lifted us up, gave good advice, and spoke positive things into the lives of so many children, especially young males. My dear mother, built strong character, and morals in us! She was a strong willed and discipline woman, who didn't take no stuff from any one of us! We all, pretty much, got everything that we could ever need. My dear mother raised five sons, worked a full-time job, cooked daily meals, kept the house clean, and did everything she possibly could do for her immediate family, as well as other family members. She did not take what some, may call, a mental health day off!

My character is my moral makeup, which helped to influence my destiny. My dear mother prepared me for the future, but I believe that my character determined how I functioned in life. It also shaped and effected my abilities that I possess inside. When we possess inner strength, we succeed, despite tough circumstances. Where we do not possess inner strength, we either get stuck or fail. My dear mother helped my brothers, and myself, develop character. This character took us through life securely, safely, and productively. We had enough instilled in us to make our future go well, despite not having a male influence in our household.

Your parent(s) or those who have formative authority in your life, speaks an identity into you. Your self-image is an impression left by others. It is not who you truly are, and it does not reflect the reality of who God created you to be. Although it is a perceived image, but for a young person, perception is reality. I believe, my problem was, that I didn't have any boundaries to follow while growing up. Having boundaries defines a person, it defines where one person ends and where the other begin. Therefore, if we know where a person's boundaries are we will be able to anticipate what they can control.

In my life, I had no boundaries, no self-control that steered me in the right direction. I was steered in the opposite direction, controlling others, and being out of control myself!

I believe this statement that came from the book, **"Boundaries with Kids"** by Dr. Cloud and Dr. Townsend, on page 18, it states **"if boundaries are clear, children develop several of the following qualities:**

- **A well – defined sense of who they are.**
- **What they are responsible for.**
- **The ability to choose.**
- **The understanding that if they choose well, things will go well, and if they choose poorly, they willsuffer.**
- **The possibility for true love is based in freedom.**

"The essence of boundaries is self-control, responsibility, freedom, and love."

When you are made to be responsible for your own actions, and not blame others or a lack of not having this or that, there is hope for self-control to develop. However, loss of self-control is seen as an increased in violence. Therefore, people struggle for power and control over their own lives and over the lives of others. People that lack self-control is most likely burdened with fear in the family, or fear of the social system. People can be motivated mainly to satisfy selfish needs, so power is used for personal advantage. Relationships are primarily exploitive!

This means making use of a situation or treating others unfairly, to gain an advantage and/or benefit from the use of people as a resource. All of this is done with little or no consideration for the well-being of others.

Again, there was no excuse for me. I continued to live the destructive lifestyle that I thought was appropriate for me. I was raised the right way, and was taught to respect my elders, as well as others. I respected my dear mother so much, therefore, I did nothing to disrespect her in front of her face. My destructive lifestyle was lived behind the scenes. She didn't know what I was doing on the streets, and I knew that she would not have approved of the lifestyle that I was living. My dear mother did not raise me to be the terror that I had become on the streets.

I wasn't raised with the help of my father. I didn't know who he was, although we had pictures of him. I had no relationship with him. Although I didn't experience any feelings of rejection, that I am aware of. Because I didn't have my father around, he was never not a part of my life. I eventually discovered that I had difficulties knowing what a wholesome (normal) relationship with someone would be.

I do strongly feel that rejection can multiply over time. Your heart and mind become groomed to fear intimacy, and you begin to look for alternative means to meet your needs. Therefore, the beginning of my story is that I began to seek pleasure in false idols. I started idolizing drugs, sex, and alcohol, and the fast-paced lifestyle of the streets.

POWER

The word on the streets was that I was a powerful force to be reckoned with, therefore, no one tried to mess with me! Power means the ability or capability to act. The basic definition includes the actual strength or force expended to do something. The meaning of power also includes the right, and capacity to exercise control, to influence, and even have dominion over someone or something. Therefore, having power or the potential of power allows you the capacity or action that can be used for good or evil, power to bless or to harm.

Power can become confused and conflicted. It is an emotional connection between those who love one another. Since it is a conflicted emotion, it allows for the potential abuse of power, leading ultimately to violence in thoughts, words, and deeds. Having such power can shift gradually and can develop into a fixation on the pleasures of life, at any cost. Caring for others became an intrusion, and a rejected nuisance. Pleasure becomes an obsession for the material things. As time passes, that obsession becomes more and more displeasing, thus eventually creating greed, frustration, and anger.

Being obsessed with pleasure devalues your view of others. It reveals a loss of empathy and a numbness toward another human being. When combined with unresolved anger and hostility, it results in increased violence. Yes, I must admit that this **_was_** me. Although I got angry in certain situations, I didn't hold on to it, nor carried it inside. Again, there were no excuses for me nor my brothers! We were raised with good morals, and the positive influences we received from our grandmother and our auntie, who was very active in our lives, and in assisting my dear mother in raising us.

I grew up not resenting my father, yet I had many questions. He didn't claim me, and he didn't want to have anything to do with me, but deep down, I had a desire to know why? I just didn't understand, how anyone could have sons, and not want to be a part of their lives? Therefore, I would constantly ask my dear mother questions, as it related to my father. She had no answers, or maybe she just didn't want to share all the answers to my questions.

Over a period, I guess my dear mother got tired of me asking so many questions about my father that, she stated to me one day, "I am your mother and your father! Don't worry I will take care of you! Everything will be alright!" My dear mother was a very giving individual.

She was a woman full of faith, strength, determination, and hard work. She was liked and highly respected by many. She went to work every day to see, not only that we were taken care of, but a lot of others in the family and in the neighborhood as well!

I did fulfill one of my dear mother's wishes, I had good grades and I managed to finish high school. I graduated from Dunbar Senior High school, located in Washington, D.C. Approximately, six months later, I was arrested and charged with 1st Degree Murder, Armored Robbery, and the use of a handgun in the commission of a felony.

Although, I did do somethings in society, because of my destructive lifestyle, I don't think I received a fair shake in court. A lot of information that pertained to my court case wasn't heard in court. If it were, I probably would not have gotten the sentence that was granted. I really had no idea why I was being arrested at the time, in the firstplace. I did not know anything about the incident in question, but somehow my name got involved.

Eventually, I later found out during a court hearing, that one of my so-called home boys had gotten arrested in Washington, D.C. for committing crimes of breaking and entering. To reduce his sentencing, he decided to squeal about an incident that took place many years before and implemented me. He told authorities about and incident, that involved a drug related murder, and included me during his account of what happened. I was arrested based on lies that he told, just to secure himself a shorter sentence, which didn't happen anyway.

Moving forward at the time of my arrest, I moved from the city of Washington, D.C. to Maryland. I lived several other places, including the state of Virginia. But on this day, I was taking my dear mother to work. When I returned home, at some time during that day, my dear mother called me. I recall talking to her on the phone, and she told me that she noticed that there was some very unusual police activity going on in our neighborhood when we were leaving out that morning.

She wanted to know if I saw anything happening in the neighborhood. Unbeknownst to me, our home was surrounded by police officers. They had positioned themselves all around the house. As I approached to look through our bay window, there was a knock at the door. My dear mother stayed on the phone with me until I answered the door. Upon opening the door, a police officer asked me, if I was Michael Stanley? I replied yes, and they told me that they had a warrant, and I was under arrest. One of the police officers, picked up the phone and told my mother that they couldn't give her any information. They informed her that I was being arrested and was being taken to the headquarters of the county jail. The officers still did not tell me what I was being arrested for, but in my mind, I thought the reason was that I had finally got caught robbing the gas station nearby. I never thought that I was being arrested for murder. My mother eventually left work and came down to the police station to see me. She didn't hesitate to tell me how disappointed, hurt, and embarrassed she was. Not to mention, the embarrassment had gotten even worst, as the news of my arrest hit the neighborhood and the eventually the local newspaper.

Anyway, back to my so-called home boy being a snitch. I was totally in shock, and I felt betrayed, but I kept my mouth shut about it. I didn't point any fingers at anyone, because where I come from, you did not snitch! You must understand that not being a snitch, was one of the first things that we learned in the streets. We practiced not snitching on anyone, no matter what! Being a snitch meant chances were that you would be branded for the rest of your life, and you would have to suffer certain consequences, as well. You were also branded as being weak; someone that couldn't handle the streets; nor the game of the streets. Snitches were known to expose any destructive activity that anyone was involved in, which would also include, what one would call "name dropping."

The minute a snitch was caught, they had to pay! It didn't matter if you were on the streets or even locked up, you were going to pay for snitching. I was a strong, young black male. I took pride, and I held my own. I refused to be a snitch! I voluntarily chose the destructive lifestyle, and what came with the territory. Therefore, the name snitch was never tied to my name. People on the streets knew that I believed in keeping my mouth shut!

This is the reason why I felt so betrayed by my so-called home boy. I just couldn't believe it! Overall keeping your mouth shut came with the territory, and as the saying goes, "snitches get stiches." But where I came from snitches got killed! My so-called home boy thought that he was going to get his sentence shorten, but he ended up pleading guilty to murder, which included in his sentencing, an increased to his prison term to approximately 30 years.

As stated previously, as it relates, to the charges brought against me, there was a lot of missing information, and some facts that did not get heard or presented on my behalf. This was coupled with lies that where told about me and my whereabouts. To top it all off, the prosecuting attorney was seeking the death penalty for me! Lord, please help me!

As it was relayed, the words on the streets, the **poison** in our minds, was that you were not a real man unless you carried a gun. If you carried one, you had better be ready to use it. Also, if you, served some time in jail, or had gone to prison, you were considered a real man! Therefore, it was a lot of negative things that were said in the streets. Things that were destructive to the mind, coupled with living in that type of negative environment, there was nothing positive. If you wanted something positive, you had to go outside of your environment, into another community or state to find it. I tried to go away into other communities, as well as my dear mother had me to relocate out of the area, to find more positive things. But when I lived in other communities, I found it very boring! Nothing compared to living in the city.

I felt that it was too late for me, and my mind was **poisoned** already. I realized that I was the by-product of a negative environment. My thought process was full of power, violence, and negativity. Therefore, the thought of going to school, and doing the right things in life, was very boring to me, and had no excitement at all for me, not by a long shot! I felt that the environment that I was raised in, was more exciting!

I lived in a project located in Washington, D.C. Therefore, I had no fear of the streets or anyone. I kept getting in trouble. My dear mother would constantly leave work because of my bad behavior. Besides, there was money, women, fancy cars, parties, pimps, and prostitutes for the picking. Again, as I stated earlier, I didn't know, that I had become a by-product of my environment and things were happening so fast around me, I barely had the opportunity to catch my breath!

It would be a serious mistake to blame the sinful choices solely on the actions of others, or my DNA. As I stated previously, I had no excuse, I was taught better! The next thing I knew I was standing before a Judge. I was in the same court room where my co-defendant, was pointing his finger at me. He testified that I was the one who pulled the trigger. This is the same guy that hung out with me and was one of the guys that I grew up with and ran the streets with. I thought he was my ride or die friend! I was shocked, hurt, angry, and betrayed!

Not to mention, that the judge had the nerve to call me a lot of low-down, dirty names. He went as far as calling me an animal. The judge stated that I was a menace to society, and that as long as he was in that position on the bench, I would never see my freedom again!

That which cometh out of the man, that defileth the man. For from within, out of the heart of men, proceed evil thoughts, adulteries, fornications, murders, thefts, covetousness, wickedness, deceit, lasciviousness, an evil eye, blasphemy, pride, foolishness: All these evil things come from within, and defile the man. **Mark 7:20-23**

MY JOURNEY TO REDEMPTION

I was a mess after getting my conviction. I had been living a destructive lifestyle for years, and it had finally caught up with me. That conviction affected me emotionally and physically. Although I enjoyed the street life, I was really run down and tired of running the streets. I ran the streets for many years. I did a lot of dirt, and I hurt so many people! My body was full of drugs and my mind was full of venom. Not to mention, I hurt my dear mother and my family.

Even after all of that, I believed that God pulled me off the streets to save my life from the streets. Let me repeat this statement. "I believe that God pulled me off the streets to save my life from the streets!" When I look back over my life, I should have been dead! Therefore, God was the *medicine* that I needed to be able to survive the next phase of my life!

I was still a young male, and I hadn't really started to live my life. I was beat down, beat up, and messed up, from the floor up! Yes, my conviction was a blessing in disguise. Being a young male assigned to a prison filled with older males, you learned to grow up very quickly! God spared my life, therefore, if I would have remained on the streets of Washington, D.C., I would have died! God saw me and He knew that I was done. I didn't know where I was going, and He stepped in. If I had remained on the streets, I would have continued with the *poison* in my mind and in my system from living in a destructive environment!

I realized then that I had to fight for my life! I had to fight through and detox my body from all my addictions as well! How in the world did my life become so unmanageable? Why did I choose such a destructive lifestyle at such a young age? I even had a child, and I didn't even know how to be a real father to my child, because I was a child myself! There was really no excuse for me! I received a lot of love from my dear mother and grandmother. They both stood in the gap and prayed for me! They never gave up on me. They saw the good in me, even when I didn't see the good in me for myself! I often asked myself why I continued to live a fascinating lifestyle in the street. I allowed myself to inhale the *poison* that penetrated my mind on a consistent basis.

What am I going to do now? I am now angry not with anyone, but myself? Here I am now sitting in prison sentenced to life plus 20 years, with no parole. Therefore, I found myself trying to figure out how in the world I was I going to get out of this? How can I make something out of my life now? How was I going to take care of my daughter? Please wake me up, from this horrific dream!!! Lord! I need you! Lord! I need you now! This was my prayer!

For the first time in my life, my thoughts became very scary to me. Sometimes God will reveal to you, who you really are to yourself! The heart can be dirty and nasty! I had to face the reality that I forfeited my life, and I had to spend the rest of my life in Prison! No more to the destructive lifestyle, so I thought…

See that none render evil, for evil unto any man; but ever follow that which is good, both among yourselves, and to all men. **I Thessalonians 5:1**

THE POISON WITHIN

I guess when the Judge called me a monster, he was right, during that time. I did a lot of things when I was a young man. Now, when I look back on them, there is nothing that I am proud of. But at that time, I didn't know that I was full of addiction and dysfunction.

Having an addiction is a very serious disease, and it robs you of your life. It also takes you to places and puts you in certain environments that you shouldn't be in. Addictions will have you dealing with people and loved ones in an erratic manner. Addiction is one of the most difficult diseases to overcome. In the process, you will hurt people and the ones that you love. Not to mention, you can have more than one addiction at one time. It is easy to have one addiction, and when that is not enough, you move on to another. When that happens, it is hard to get it under control.

Everything that I did, every crime that I committed, I did while under the influence of something. Not only did I sell drugs, but I was also heavy on several drugs myself. My addiction started with marijuana (weed), and then when marijuana wasn't enough, I started lacing it with cocaine. Then one day I was introduced to free-basing cocaine, and that is when my addiction took off! I kept chasing and running after the drugs. At the same time, I was also addicted to alcohol and sex. Therefore, I was chasing after that as well. My life became so unmanageable, and I was a total mess!

I had no respect or serious interest in having a relationship with girls or anyone at that time. I started my downhill journey at the age of 13 years old, and the older that I got, the more I got involved with addictions. I wanted what I wanted, and I did everything to get what I wanted!

I loved the drugs, sex, and alcohol. Sex was sex, and I didn't think of the consequences of my actions. The idea of making a baby or the thought of any diseases that came with having unprotected sex, was never a fleeting thought. Therefore, it came back to bite me. I got someone pregnant, and I had also become infected with sexual transmitted diseases as well, during my many sexual encounters.

Drugs and alcohol went hand in hand, and being addicted made me feel good and bad, in my body, at the same time. Having my head clouded with those substances, allowed me to do terrible and unforgivable things to people. I craved these addictions, as well as the streets.

I can remember one time in my life, I was so heavy on drugs that I left home, and I took a man's wife! Yes! Many of us back then that were on the streets, were heavy on drugs. We were so heavy on drugs that we would do almost anything for drugs. Once, this man traded his wife for drugs that I was selling, because he didn't have the money to buy them. The man's words were "you can do whatever you want with my wife" and he left! I never saw him again, and I moved in with his wife who was also heavy on drugs. We both did drugs quite frequently. I lost so much weight. I believe that I weighed about 130 lbs., which is very skinny for a man with a height of 5'11.

At this time in my life, I stayed away from my family, and I didn't want to be seen by any of them. I didn't want my family to see me in the bad state that I was in either! I didn't even look in the mirror because I didn't want to see myself. I also can remember during that time, several times a week, my dear mother would come by to check on me. She would call me from the outside, and I would just wave my arm out of the window so that she would know that I was ok. My dear Mother would then proceed to leave food at the front door to make sure that I had something to eat. There were times that I couldn't remember if I ate or not. That is what addictions can do to you. The addictions that I had, destroyed the beginning of my life. Eventually I had to accept that I lost a lot of time in life that I will never get back!

One day I finally looked at myself in the mirror! I was a terrible mess, and I did not know who this guy was looking back at me! The sad thing is that I never knew that I was addicted. To me my dysfunctional lifestyle was normal. I now realize, and I accept, that I came from a very dysfunctional family, and this bothers me to the point that it hurts! I know that I can't save everybody, but I want to save my family from these generational curses of addictions. My hope is that we will be closer and be there for one another.

I want my family to forgive me for the things that I have done! I have also learned to accept that some family members, as well as others may refuse to allow me to help them. I know that I have a very strong and aggressive personality. I am known to keep things real, and I say what is on my mind. Therefore, if you don't want to hear the truth, don't ask me! I keep it real! Some people can't handle the truth, and I must admit that I need to learn how to be careful in my approach in speaking the truth. I understand also that some people have not forgiven me or are still holding me hostage to my past mistakes. Therefore, they don't understand me being candid about addictions, dysfunctional lifestyles, and anyone having a love for what are **lies** on the streets, even though I lived through that type of lifestyle.

I am full of compassion for helping those that may not see the destruction that they are headed towards. People that knew the old me, also feel that I can't tell them anything. They don't see that I am a different person, a changed man that has been broken and transformed. Not perfect! Not by a long shot! Do I still make mistakes? Yes! I am not the young, in-mature, stupid, Sweet Tooth that I use to be. God is still transforming me to be wiser, and greater, and to impact the lives of anyone that I meet. My life now is of God, and I have a purpose and call on my life!

The more I try to help others, I see that people will still hold your past against you. People just won't believe that you can recover and change your life for the better! I am so grateful that God isn't like people! God knows my heart. He forgave me from all my addictions and the crimes that I committed while under the influence of my addictions. Every day that I wake up, I thank God that

He has allowed me to breath, see, smell, feel, taste, and to walk in total freedom and love. Each day I have on this earth is a chance that God allows me to get it right. I am still a work in progress. If I feel that I can help just one person at a time, I have fulfilled the purpose that God has upon my life! I may not be perfect, but I am a better person than I was before! I know that I stated this previously, but it is worth repeating. I thank God for loving me and giving me grace! I am a voice of experience!

Although people can hold you hostage to your past, God won't! I lost many years in life, but God promised me in His word that he will restore me and give me back the years that I thought that I had lost.

And I will restore to you the years that the locust has eaten, the cankerworm, and the caterpillar, and the palmerworm. **Joel 2:2**

BEING INCARCERATED

The first couple of years, while being incarcerated, were one on the hardest years for me! The realization of being incarcerated was no joke! I had to face all my indiscretions, deal with myself, and all of my addictions.

I stated earlier that I was given the nickname "Sweet Tooth" at the young age of 8, by our neighbors that I ran errands for. His wife was pregnant at the time. Every time I ran errands for them, there was always a little extra change left over for me to have. I loved candy and I would buy candy with the change that was left over. One day my neighbor stated to me, "I am going to call you, "Sweet Tooth," because, boy! You eat a lot of candy!

That name stuck and became the name that everyone knew me by on the streets. And still today, people from my old neighborhood identify me with that name. Can you imagine going into the prison system with a nickname like that? Of course, you can't! Mind-boggling!

There were so many degrading nicknames in prison that was directed to homosexuality. There were many young men from my hometown, that was incarcerated already, who knew me by my street name. On my way to prison, I remembered riding the bus. When I got there, and got off the bus, one of my homeboys called out, "Hey Sweet Tooth!" Boy you finally made it here!? Within ears reach, I heard another guy call out, and he said, "Hey when you're finished with "sweet a**," send him down here to me, because I want to do somethings to him!" You can imagine the "somethings" that he was referring to. Right at that present moment, it started a rage within me, and made for a rough ride on my first day of entry into the prison system.

Immediately, once I entered prison, I was given a knife. I proceeded to go find the guy who made the smart, degrading remarks. I didn't take kindly to someone making homosexual propositions toward me. I am not a homosexual! Therefore, someone would have to kill me to try to violate me, and I was not going to allow anyone to do that to me! I was going to show this guy that I was a force, to be reckoned with! I had to show that to everyone in the prison, who even thought of putting their hands on me!

Besides, I am a strong, and tough, a ladies' man! I was full of rage, and I wanted to get to this guy. Thank God, the guards in the prison, came in time, and prevented me from killing him. I didn't hit any major arteries, but they had to fly him to shock trauma. Therefore, I was immediately sent to a special place in the prison, called super maximum for what I did to him.

The place that I once lived

SUPER MAX

Super Max is a higher punishment for inmates that manly commit horrific crimes against prison staff or other inmates, while incarcerated.

A normal prisoners' daily life is established based on a rigid schedule. There are scheduled times to wake-up, there are roll-calls, morning exercises, specific times for meals, and times established for escorting prisoners to work and school. There are also times for studying and working, as well as, times that are prescribed for sporting events, telephone calls, walks, and church services.

In Super Max, you are locked down 24 hours a day. You may shower once a week, if that, and you cannot have visits with anyone for the first 30 days. You are given three meals daily. However, if you commit an infraction while in super max, your meal for dinner is made up with the many different types of food that they serve throughout the day. This food is mixed all together and baked, into what appears to look like somewhat of a meatloaf. It's then sliced, and served to you, and the taste was something horrible! I wouldn't have served my dog a meal like this! In fact, dogs would not have liked such a meal!

When I got to Super Max, there were many other inmates that had already been assigned there for quite some time. In Super Max, you were deprived of everything, not to mention, they continued to inflict some type of psychological pain on you! Talk about locking you up and throwing away the key. They did just that! You really had to have a strong mind and a strong will to live. Therefore, some didn't make it out of super max, psychologically, their minds were gone! You come in one way, but you don't leave out the same.

DISCIPLINARY SEGREGATION AND SOLITARY CONFINEMENT

Disciplinary Segregation, which is sometimes referred to as, "the hole," is a form of separation from the general population for a specified period. The Discipline Hearing Officer, (DHO), orders disciplinary segregation for inmates who have committed any violations of the Bureau of Prisons. Inmates assigned to Disciplinary Segregation are isolated from the general population. They receive services and activities separate from the other inmates. Extreme isolation refers to situations where inmates are seen by other staff or other inmates fewer than three times a day.

Solitary Confinement or Administrative Segregation is used when prisoners are deemed a risk to the safety of other inmates or prison staff. You are confined to an individual cell for 24 hours a day, except for showers. You are not permitted to work or have any visitation and even canteen access is restricted.

Mr. Craig Haney, who is an American Social Psychologist and a professor at the University of California, Santa Cruz, who is noted for his work on the study of capital punishment and the psychological impact of imprisonment and prison isolation since the 1970s. His study details, the risks of Solitary Confinement. Mr. Haney, stated that, "One of the very serious psychological consequences of solitary confinement, is that it renders many people incapable of living anywhere else." He also stated that, when prisoners are released into regular cells, or back into society, they are often overwhelmed with anxiety.

Therefore, going back into society can be overwhelming, and you still must face other people who treat you like dirt! Your chances of having a normal life are slim. Who will give you chance? Will they make you suffer, because of your past? Can there be a change in you? This answer to all these questions is yes!

Being incarcerated, was one of the most difficult times of my destructive life. I was so young, and I had not quite started to live my life! Therefore, mentally, I was in a dark place. My cell had very, very bright lights that stayed on 24 hours a day. It was their way to inflict more punishment on you psychologically. This was done so that you would not be able to sleep. The only way to communicate to the prison staff, was through a little door that had a latched on it. Through that same little door is where you got served your meals. At times that same little door, was used by inmates, who would try to stick their arms out of the door to feel the air outside of the cell, or to touch a prison officer, in order to get some type of physical attention. In some cases, the prison officers had to almost break an inmates' arm to get their arm back into the cell.

The front of your cell was blocked with plexi-glass. Since the plexi-glass was so old, over a period of time, you couldn't see clearly through it. At times, you would hear other inmates talking to themselves or hollering out loud. There were the nasty inmates as well, that would defecate in a tube or bottle and splatter it through the vent in the cell next to them, or they would throw it out of the little door on a prison officer.

I literally thought I would lose my mind! I really didn't know how I was going to make it! I had to think positive things, and rely totally, on my relationship with God to get me though this.

George Jackson, who was one of the Black Panthers, made a statement, "Prison requires minimum adjustment, because this is how we lived in the ghetto, the slums, and the projects." I can truly relate to this statement, because that is what I saw in the streets, where I lived. This was certainly not the case in Solitary Confinement that was a different story!

I must admit that in the projects, we lived with roaches, we lived with mice and a lot of things in the household were broken and did not work. Therefore, when I got to prison, there were many of the same things. We still had the roaches, mice, fussing, fighting, and everyone jockeying for a position.

I was put away in Solitary Confinement for four years. At first, it was scary, and my mind was in a very dark place. I had to deal with my addictions and bad habits totally by myself. After being isolated for some time, that feeling lost its intimidation. As the month and years passed, and the older I got, I came to grips with the fact that I had to be there. I realized that I had to suffer and pay for the crimes that I had done, not the crime that I was initially convicted for. Days were long and seemed like it lasted forever. I never knew what time it was, what day it was, if it was night or day, nor what month or year it was. I lost myself in time!

My time in isolation took away all my cravings for all the addictions that I had. It was during that time that I had made up in my mind that I was never ever going to smoke weed, do drugs or alcohol again! I also learned that once your body was detoxed from any addictions, you cannot do anything to trigger or entertain any past addiction. Besides many didn't have a chance to get to know the real me, Michael, without any addictions. I too, had lost sight of him. I was known by the name Sweet Tooth, in the streets and in prison. Therefore, who was Michael W. Stanley? I had to get to know, my true self, and know who God was also. Besides, God was all I had!

I finally woke up and got my mind together, because I realized that I could not change a thing. I learned to cope by sleeping, reading, praying, and trusting in God, I also used my time to encourage the inmates that were on each side of me. I found ways to stay up all night and sleep all day. What really got me through some tough moments, was my relationship that I was building with God. Realizing that I had to change my way of thinking. I relied on God.

God injected me with the *medicine* of His love, His word, and His spirit! I started learning and hearing from God. We had a relationship, and I could totally depend on Him! I started thinking that this situation too, shall pass. I also started thinking about the positive support team that I had in several members of my family. I only had a few of my family members that supported and believed in me. I was grateful that they didn't turn their backs on me, some did! I finally, was able to receive mail while in solitary confinement. That was the only form of contact I had with my dear mother. She wrote me often, and her letters where very uplifting and encouraging. When I wrote back, I found that it was very relieving. At times, being isolated, became unbearable. There were some inmates that worried so much that they didn't eat. At times, I was one of them, I had my moments.

The food was horrible and our time scheduled to eat was, like... 5am breakfast, 10am lunch, 3pm dinner, which was your last meal until 5am the next day. I lost approximately 20 pounds or more while in solitary confinement. Solitary Confinement really takes a toll on you psychologically. You do lose yourself in time, but it didn't beat me! I overcame one of the most challenging times of my life. Thanks to God!

GOD BROUGHT ME THROUGH

Eventually the end of my four years came, and my time in Solitary Confinement was done. It felt like ten years to me, but thank God, He bought me through! God injected the *medicine* that I needed in me, so that I could survive in this place!

Once I got out of Solitary Confinement that was the beginning of my normal life in prison life. Again, I was highly respected, and the other inmates looked up to me and made me a hero. Yes, in prison! Because of stabbing someone and spending four years in Solitary Confinement. Who would have thought that you would be given such respect and a title, in a prison? It came with the territory, but that tells you the mindset of the men that were incarcerated. I was happy to be out of Solitary Confinement and I just didn't want anyone to bother me or think that they could control me! Truth be told, once I got out of Solitary Confinement, I was very paranoid for a period of time. I had to adjust to becoming a part of the prison population. I had to learn how to interact with people, because I was alone for four years in my cell.

The news, of my prison experience was heard

throughout the prison. Stories of what I did were told, by old and new inmates. It rang out throughout the prison! Do not to mess with "Sweet Tooth" or you would get a knife in you! That statement was tied to my name, therefore, that story was carried about me throughout my whole time of incarceration. My story kept any inmates from thinking that they could mess with me. Therefore, my story protected me while I was incarcerated.

I was incarcerated in a state penitentiary. Many of the inmates were born and raised in a nearby city or state. Once I got assigned there, it was obvious that the inmates that were there, did not care much for the inmates that were from certain other areas. The inmates that were from the nearby city, felt that anyone coming in, were on their turf. They felt that we were in their city, and on their territory, now what? This attitude triggered more disagreements, more threats, fights, and other things that you had to do to protect yourself being in that environment.

As time went on, ***_real_*** men started to respect each other. Therefore, many men developed, a level of respect towards each other. At some point, we all felt that we were going to be incarcerated for a very long time, so we had to stick together and look out for one another. In all, only the strong survived! If you were a weak man, chances were that you were going to be taken advantage of, and that you probably were not going to survive! The penitentiary was difficult, and it was a mess!

For I know the plans I have for you Declares the Lord, plans to prosper You and not to harm you, plans to give you hope and a future. **Jeremiah 29:1**

SEX AND HOMOSEXUALITY IN THE PRISON

If you were deemed a weak man, you became another man's girlfriend. Many weak men got raped and were forced to participate in homosexual acts. Some men that were "strong" even turned to a homosexual lifestyle, to obtain favors. Some even felt that they had no other choice if they wanted to stay alive or be protected. There were gangs in the prison, just like it was on the street. Prior to me getting assigned to the penitentiary, I was assigned into the Diagnostic Area. Diagnostic was a building nearby, basically, a holding cell, where you stayed, until they assigned you to your destination. While there, we were permitted to do work releases, and there was minimum security, medium security, or maximum security at that site. Anyway, while I was assigned in Diagnostic, I was already told that, the nearby state penitentiary where I was headed to was called a "freak house." Basically, all kinds of sexual perversion were going on in that penitentiary.

It was unfortunate being in a confined population where males had very high sexual needs. With their high sexual desire, inmates were either going to take it from another inmate, by force or else! You don't want to know what the "or else" happened to be. Anyway, I witnessed, and at times, heard the cries of men that got raped. I also heard men ask other inmates to participate in homosexual acts. Gay men were already coming into the prison system and knew that the only way to survive was to hook up with other inmates and become what some called their "b*tch." Therefore, no other inmate would bother them because they "belonged" to someone else. There were also inmates that was primarily around just to have sex with other inmates. They felt that if there was any way to get their sexual needs met they were going to do it. We had a name for them also. In fact, there were some ministers that would come into the prison for church services, but they would push up on the inmates for sexual favors also. This was very upsetting to me, and it made me sick to my stomach! This made me not want to participate in any church services, because I felt that I couldn't trust the system that was set in place for worship.

Nevertheless, I don't have to say to anyone, that NO ONE BOTHERED ME at all, especially as it relates, in that manner! If you want to know why or forgot, go back, and read the pervious pages!

There were all kinds of sexual acts going on in the

Prison. What I heard before I got there, was the truth!

Therefore, some of the men that you thought were straight or held leadership positions within the penitentiary turned out to be involved in homosexual acts as well. You could not trust anyone!

Diagnostic Center

Michael W. Stanley

There were correctional officers as well, that were gay, or bisexual and they performed sexual acts with inmates behind closed doors. At times there were also female prostitution going on as well. There were female officers having sex with inmates in exchange for money or special favors.

I remember once there were approximately nine women outside of the prison that we were having conversations with us through a window. We referred to the place where we were standing as the "catwalk", which allowed us to look out onto the street. Eventually these women connected with a few of the inmates and were able to come into the penitentiary to attend a couple social functions. I wanted to be a part of the fun as well. Nevertheless, for some apparent reason, I was not chosen to be a part of the fun with these ladies. As time went on, many of the inmates that were involved with some of the women, ended up HIV positive, and a few of the inmates eventually passed away. I thank God that He protected me from death! God was undeniable on my side, and He protected me from the evil things that was going on in the prison, even when I wanted to be a part of the action! Again, as I stated previously, you cannot entertain past addictions, and sex was one of mine. Therefore, I believe that if I had entertained my addiction at that time, it would have cost me my life!

Like I stated previously, everything that you could get off the streets, you could also get inside of the prison. The questions were, how did you get it and who did you got it from?

The penitentiary was a run down, dirty place. It had been deemed condemned many times while we were there. The officials did not care about us at all. Some of the comments made by them were: *"Let the place cave in! These guys are the worst of the worst!"* *Who cares about these guys*!

COLLEGE

Moving forward, I have always been an advocate for education, even when I didn't take it seriously myself. I guess my dear mother pounded it so much in my mind as a kid. She also knew that I was no dummy.

I eventually went back to further my education and enrolled in Coppin State College. There were representatives that came to the prison to recruit new students under the Pell Grant, and I was one of them that jumped at the opportunity. I started attending college in the year 1988 and finished in 1992. I graduated with a Bachelor of Science Degree (BS) in Applied Psychology, Magna Cum Laude. My family was in attendance, as I walked across the stage at the graduation ceremony. I really felt good about myself that day. That was not my first nor my last major accomplishment.

In the year 1993, they cut the Pell Grant. Therefore, a lot of the inmates did not benefit from the paid opportunity to go to college. They lost the opportunity by not enrolling in college when they had a chance. Some inmates felt they had all the time in the world to apply to college. Therefore, they missed a great opportunity to get a free education. You also had some that may have started a semester or two but did not continue. Others attended college for a year and/or dropped out eventually. They got caught without furthering their education. For me, that was the best decision I could have ever made. I felt good about my decisions and my accomplishments!

Shortly after obtaining my degree, I became one of the first founders of the penitentiary's first counseling center.

The counseling center was started to help, advise, and give counsel to new inmates, who entered the prison system, and that could not find their way emotionally. It was very difficult for them to adjust. They had difficulty facing the reality of not having any freedom and learning their new way of life. There were other counselors besides me. We were there to help them learn to cope, while being incarcerated. We assisted them in getting work, getting their G.E.D., if they didn't have a high school diploma, etc. The counselors also recommended, facilitated, and referred inmates into self- help groups. These groups assisted the inmates when they needed further counseling or therapy.

One thing that I learned while being incarcerated, is that the prison is designed to *destroy you, mentality, and is also designed to keep you coming back*! Of course, you must serve the time you were given, but the system is designed to keep you coming back! A repeat offender! It isn't designed to help you cope, get you through the battles in your mind, nor get you through life's challenges! It is also not designed to provide needed education and to establish you as a person prepared to re-enter society. There are no positive things or influences there at all! You had to come up with positive things on your own or build a connection with someone that was positive. Drugs were still prevalent, alcohol, and homosexuality were all still prevalent as well. In fact, all the things that was done on the outside, you could continue to do on the inside!

The men that had the destructive influence on the outside, had the destructive influence on the inside.

Michael W. Stanley

I graduated with a Bachelor of Science Degree (BS) in Applied Psychology, Magna Cum Laude

TRANSFORMATION

Being placed behind bars is a form of death! The *poison* and mental torture that seeps in the mind is also a mental death! Because of how God has ordered my steps and kept me. I have been transformed. I believe that God's purpose was more powerful in me, than the pain that I was experiencing behind bars.

I started my prison journey with an entirely different mindset on things, and on life itself. I gambled with my life and took it for granted. To make the change needed in my life, I had to go through a total transformation, which had to start with the renewing of my mind! After spending fifteen years in prison, one would say that "the light bulb came on!". "God showed up!" God renewed my mind and placed me on a street called "straight." I no longer wanted to live the destructive lifestyle! The hungers and thirsts that I had for the streets left! I wanted to live and not die! I wanted a better life and a second chance! I prayed and I asked God to give me another chance at life. I vowed that I wouldn't do anything that would put me back in that terrible situation again. I knew that God had not forsaken me, and that He had something that He wanted me to do for the kingdom! We serve a mighty and awesome God who answers prayers! God answered my prayers! The *poison* left my mind, and God became the *medicine* that I needed to survive and complete my transformation as a renewed person!

Where does transformation start? One doesn't think about transformation unless something is broken; it could be damaged in many ways, defeated, dejected, dispirited, or just overpowered! Transformation is usually the steps required to fix or repair something that was broken. Something must be broken or require change or a makeover. In our brokenness, if we call upon the Lord for help, God heals and changes us.

The Lord is near to the brokenhearted, and saves those who are crushed in spirit. **Psalms 34:18**

My grace is sufficient for thee: for my strength is made perfect in weakness. **2 Corinthians 12:9**

We must allow God to deal with the hidden roots of sin within our own hearts. For out of the heart flows the issues of life. When ministering to those in need, we must believe that they too can change, and that their lives can be transformed.

Many of our hearts has never been given over to God or the things of God. Many of us have never dealt with the things of the heart, except in a negative way. God wants our hearts healed, and the church in us to be purified.

Change must first start within your heart. There must be ways of inner sanctification and transformation. It is a necessity! You must dedicate your heart to God's will and God's way and devote your time to praying and studying His word. The Lord heals; therefore, we must have confidence, and rest in his ability to keep us, and not us to rely on our own character or our own understanding. We are healed by being taught to put no confidence whatsoever in our own flesh, but to rest in God!

For we are the true circumcision, who worship in the Spirit of God. **Philippians 3:3**

We tend to have grounds for confidence in the flesh if we were pursuing salvation by works. One cannot achieve salvation in his own efforts. Therefore, we are clothed with the righteousness of Jesus, and Jesus alone, destroys the power of our control and brings us under subjection to His will and His way. We die to our sins when we receive salvation and are then made a new creature in Christ.

Therefore, we are clothed with the righteousness of Jesus. Jesus alone, destroys the power of our control, and brings us under subjection to His will and His way. We die to our sins when we receive salvation and are then made a new creature in Christ.

The transformation and renewing of our minds, does not fully reform our flesh. The things that I considered advancements or of high regard when I was still doing the things of the world, are now considered absolutely worthless! I gave up those things for the sake of Christ and the purpose which He has given my life. I have given up on the things of the world so that I may gain a life of Christ.

Psychologists could guide us and encourage us enough to restore our self-images so that we would regain confidence, respect, and appreciation for ourselves. But in Jesus the Christ, He would destroy, all our fleshly self-confidence (old man) so that our true, Godly, only self-image/esteem can become new (new man)!

A self-image is something we build, in which we falsely learn to trust, and having a self-image sets us into being self-centered. When we are self-centered, we have a manufactured or planned self-image. As a result of that, we strive to live up to our hype, striving to and make sure others see us and reward us, according to the image we portray and have created for ourselves. No! This is not necessary! A Christian's identity is a gift that God puts in us, and it does not necessarily have to be seen, rewarded, or defended. However, whatever sin character we have developed, whether good or bad, we must die to sin and be transformed in Jesus Christ.

I can do all things through Christ which strengthenth me. **Philippians 4:13**

Michael W. Stanley

God transformed my life. I now stand from the outside looking at a place that I once knew. I currently use my voice of experience to keep the youth from a life in prison.

SELF-IMAGE

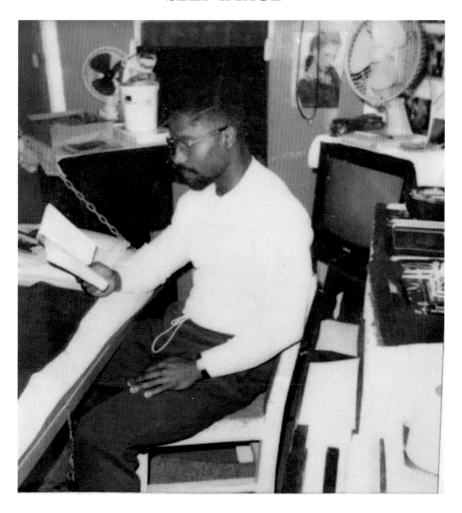

I love to read, and this is one of the things I loved to do to improve my self-image. (Me in my cell)

How do you view yourself? Do you see yourself the way God sees you? In a book, by Josh McDowell, entitled"His Image…My Image," defines three basic emotional needs that are common to all persons:

• The need to feel loved, accepted; to have a sense of belonging.
• The need to feel acceptable; to have a sense of worthiness.
• The need to feel adequate; to have a sense of competence.

Mr. McDowell, states further in his book, something one should all consider, he stated that "The problem with basing our self-image on any one of the three areas is that we use that one area to justify the others." Unfortunately, this does not work. We tend to set up one, or even two, areas as a defensive strategy against the other one. We maintain our defense strategy to cover up what we feel is the real, and the truth about ourselves."

As we look at the process of rebuilding our self-image and our relationships, we must keep in mind that we cannot disperse in *a day* what has accumulated over a lifetime. The process of rebuilding takes time, and one must work out in the flesh, what has already been accomplished in the Spirit.

Many of the false notions one thinks of himself are lies that are planted by the enemy. We must replace the lies with the truth of God's Word! The truth is that we are loved by God and were chosen by Him from the foundation of the world. The Holy Spirit will help one to expose the lies and help you to root out all the lies that the enemy embedded in you about yourself.

To the praise of the glory of his grace, wherein he hath made us accepted in the beloved. **Ephesians 1:6**

True sanctification and transformation cannot be fully accomplished in the Body of Christ, unless we start to minister to the inner man; it is a vital key to the transformation of the hearts of every normal Christian! One must understand that transformation will require more than just accepting Christ as Lord and Savior. One must learn to apply the *cross of Christ* through prayer, and counsel to the sinful structures that was built into your heart over a lifetime.

We find ourselves wrestling internally, no matter what realities we face in our lives. It doesn't matter, whether it's pleasant, routine, horrifying, and/or traumatic. We usually don't share with others the way we wrestle with sin, pain, fear, and anger. We would rather avoid the internal trails we are coping with, but that can't help or reduce the raging emotions we feel within. Therefore, we must get beyond them; not around them, but through them. There is hope in God, and several other approaches we can use in dealing with our problems.

Our hope in God helps us get beyond our issues and step up to bigger and more eternal things which transcends our thoughts, and hearts.

"We love, because He first loved us. If someone says, 'I love God; and hate his brother, he is a liar; for the one who does not love his brother whom he has seen, cannot love God whom he has not seen. This commandment we have from Him, that the one who loves God should love his brother also." **I John 4:19-21**

Evangelism is the primary way to all sanctification and transformation and the Lord must be allowed to occupy the inner space in a believer's heart.

THE POWER OF TRANSFORMATION

The power for change according to psychologists, is found in the natural desire and the human will power of the person seeking help. These factors coupled, with the support of relatives and friends, plus counsel, are additional keys to change, according to most psychologist. But God gives us alternatives for change through the basic key to life in the Ten Commandments and in the Sermon on the Mount.

ACHIEVING TRANSFORMATION

We must make every attempt to recognize our "sinful performance orientation." When did it begin, and when did it start becoming a part of your lifestyle? When did you start adapting to your new sin lifestyle? You must pay careful attention to becoming comfortable and acclimated to that lifestyle. Once you have adapted that "sinful orientation", it is not easy to change, because evil practices of the flesh become inbred and are stubborn, and hard to get rid of.

"Wherefore seeing we also are compassed about with so great a cloud of witnesses, let us lay aside every weight, and the sin which doth so easily beset us, and let us run with patience the race that is set before us, Looking unto Jesus the author and finisher of our faith; who for the joy that was set before him endured the cross, despising the shame, and is set down at the right hand of the throne of God." **Hebrews, 12:1**

SANCTIFICATION

The Bible teaches that we are all born sinners with the sinful, selfish natures. Unless we are born again by the Spirit of God, we will never see the kingdom of God (**John 3:3**).

We are born with a sinful nature, and we inherited it from Adam. Every one of us was affected by Adam's sin; there are no exceptions. We are born sinners, and for that reason we are unable to do good in order to please God in our natural state, or the flesh.

He made Him who knew no sin to be sin on our behalf that we might become the righteousness of God. Because we are born sinners, we must experience a second, spiritual birth. We are born once, into Adam's family, and are sinners by nature. When we are born again, we are born into God's family and are given the nature of Christ. We can be born again and receive salvation according to Romans 10:9. God's nature outshines and glorifies us though all our brokenness. Jesus was the perfect sacrifice for our sins.

Therefore, we must also take up our own cross daily to continue to slaughter our old man. In doing this, our daily walk will replicate God's walk for our life. We will sanctify our lives by doing God's will and doing it God's way. Our natural man will be edified, and our faith will increase. In doing this process, each of us can build a "self" we can accept. We must accept ourselves the way we are in Jesus and allow him to express his goodness and righteousness in us through the Holy Spirit.

Come as you are! We are already accepted, right where we are, as we are. The Lord's love is unconditional. He will build us! Therefore, the Lord wants us to accept us as we are, whether we are rotten, confused, or unchanged, and He then wants us to let Him express His goodness and righteous in us, through His Holy Spirit!

BACK IN THE COURTROOM

After going back to court several times, it cost my family a lot of money. After I went to court the third time, I had to get a public defender to represent me. For some apparent reason, I was always in the same court room as in previous times, for my hearings. This same public defender was appointed to represent me again, and again. Each time, I lost the hearing using him.

Another Public Defender, approached my dear mother after one of my hearings, and told her that she wanted to take my case and defend me. The public defender had previously gathered all the information that was related to my case. I had no idea that she met with my dear mother until after I was transported back to prison.

I can remember leaving the court room on that day and headed back to prison. I looked at my dear mother's face, Icouldn't say anything to her face to face, but I wished that she could have read my mind. In my mind I told my dear mother, that we had to keep our spirits up, and everything was going to be alright. I just felt it in my spirit!

Later, my dear mother shared with me the news about the Public Defender with me. Not only did she want to represent me, but she was willing to take on my case for free! Praise God! Soon thereafter, The Public Defender sent me some paperwork for me to sign to release me from my previous representative, so that she could take on my case.

Moving forward, back at the prison. I got into another altercation and was sent to Eastern Correctional Institution. While I was there in lock up I received some paperwork from the Public Defender to fill out and send back to her. I later received a letter, sometime around my birthday, from the Public Defender again, this time, stating that she would represent me, and that she would talk to a Judge on my behalf. By this time, I had been incarcerated for approximately twenty-seven years. Not to mention, approximately ninety days prior to getting that letter, and because of my altercation with an individual, I received the good news while in lockup.

I AM FREE!
THANK GOD! I AM FREE!!

In April, sometime near my birthday, I received a letter which caught me by surprise! Happy Birthday to me! I couldn't believe my eyes! The letter that I received was to inform me that the court agreed to my request to be released from prison. The court hearing was scheduled on my actual birthday. My sentence, to *life* with twenty years and no parole, will no longer be in effect! Hallelujah!

During my court hearing I was told that I had served twenty-seven years and with the time I had served, I would be eligible for an immediate release! Praise God! I was so excited! I was beside myself, overjoyed, elated! God gave me another chance, another opportunity to get it right! God answered my prayers, and my dear mother's prayers!

Shortly after that, I was transferred to a new prison. During that time there, I worked in the Gym for approximately one week. One day I got a call to report to my unit. I had a gut feeling – a feeling in my spirit, that it was the call for me to leave, but I played it cool. Therefore, when I got back to my unit, I was advised to pack up all of my things, and that it was time for me to leave the premises. I didn't have anything to pack, because I had given all I had to the other inmates for them to enjoy.

I was so excited to be leaving prison after being there for so many years! The journey of living a destructive lifestyle is that there is no good end. Your only options become going to prison, being placed an institution, or death! I no longer wanted such a life! I wanted to start my life fresh and new!

I played a destructive game with my life and I almost lost! But the God that I serve, is a Mighty Wonderful God! I thank Him for taking me off the streets at an early age. This may have protected me from the destructive lifestyle that I was living and allowed me an opportunity to reflect and to see, the destructive life that I had to leave behind! He allowed me to redeem myself and become a positive, and productive member of society. Some of the men from the streets, did not get another chance, nor did not make it. But Thank God, I was one of the one's who did! Thank God!

One that is striving to be what one is supposed to be is a far cry from becoming what God intends when we are transformed. Transformation starts from the inside out.

Yet this inner transformation is always a resistance for a variety of reasons. We must give away being in our own strength to submit to the power of Our Lord and Savior Jesus Christ by putting all our trust in His plan for our lives.

When we possess inner strength, we succeed, often despite tough circumstances. Where we don't possess inner strength, we get stuck, or we fail. Our failures could come through, the loss of time, the loss of things that we enjoy or the people that we value. We may lose freedom, and/or life itself. When a person sows' irresponsibility, they will reap the consequences. Don't forget the saying… you reap what you sow. This is where true change in a person's behavior takes place. This happens after they encounter the "reality" of their consequences, for not being responsible. If you sow good deeds, you will reap good deeds and vice versa.

One must learn to have respect for others. They must respect their existence, needs, choices, and feelings, and learn to not be hurtful to others. One must respect limits and boundaries in life and do the right things, for the right reasons.

Michael W. Stanley

Be not deceived; God is not mocked: for whatsoever a man soweth, that shall he also reap. For he that soweth to his flesh shall of the flesh reap corruption; but he that soweth to the Spirit shall of the Spirit reap life everlasting. And let us not be weary in well doing: for in due season we shall reap, if we faint not. **Galatians 6:7**

BACK INTO SOCIETY
RECIDIVISM

In 2007 case study, known collectively as the "pains of imprisonment" they argued that there are five fundamental deprivations, which are characterized daily from prison life. Those deprivations include, the loss of liberty, having access to desirable goods and services, having the lack of heterosexual relationships, having autonomy, and ample security. Therefore, former inmates, are not able to cope with being placed back into society, as a result, they fall into what's called recidivism. This means that they may backslide or become "repeat offenders."

Being introduced back into society is difficult. After the excitement of being free in this world wears off, reality sets in. What am I going to do next? How will I start to build my life? First you try to learn about everything that you missed. You start to enjoy life, and you also try to build relationships that you may have lost with family and friends. One of the most disappointing things is the fact that no one trust you. Trust is something that you earn, but some people close the door and lock it or will not allow you to earn their trust. It is as if they hold you hostage to your past mistakes. I can remember holding a job at a certain center, where there was a certain amount of money taken. I was the first person that got accused of taking the money. The director of that center falsely accused me and fired me! I was so hurt, that I literally cried and begged to keep my job. Eventually, there was more money stolen from that center and it was later discovered that a person that worked in administration was stealing the money.

Yes, my first couple of years back into society wasn't easy, but with the help of my dear mother I made it. I was allowed to move at a moderate pace until I got myself together. Although my body was detoxed from the addictions that I had, I had one addiction that still lingered, and that was sex! I was running rapid when it came to women. I didn't want a serious relationship with anyone! All I wanted was sex! Believe it or not, some women that I met also only wanted sex, and it was like I became a sex object to them. Some women were even a lot older than me, and I entertained that as well. It also became easy for me because women were coming after me. Believe it or not, I turned some women down for coming on to me! I was also approached by several women who were in the church, who had refrained from having sex, and I jumped on that opportunity as well. I also tried to build serious relationships, but they never worked! Like I stated, it was only about sex! I messed up many women's lives, and hurt several people, all because of my past sexual addiction.

Breaking that sex addiction was challenging and required strict discipline. For many years, and even recently, I have worked through that brutal compulsion of sex addiction. Through all my perseverance, I have learned to build a trusting and loving relationship, without sex being a part of the relationship.

Since being back in Society, my number one goal and passion is allowing my gifts and talents to be used in the things that I do with the "work of my hands." …With the help of God. I will continue to use the lessons learned from my own personal experiences, to show, teach, and try to influence the lives of young women and men of today. My main purpose is to reach back into the community and motivate the youth of today in hope of guiding them into a positive lifestyle.

I use my influence and my testimony to show, and teach them, that I am proof that living a destructive lifestyle does not work! I try to steer them from going down the destructive road. I impress upon them, that the destructive road, it is not the road to take, and in the long run, it does not work! No matter how big and bad, you may think that you are! I try to convey that, they will be playing Russian and Roulette with their lives, and they may not make it! If you are given better alternatives, why play with or gamble with your life, and with your future?

It has been a long difficult journey for me, but I hung in there. I believed God, and He is the source of my strength! It has now been close to twenty years of my total release, and over forty years of sobriety. Every day, I thank God for waking me up, and giving me another chance at life! He was the *medicine* that I needed to survive!

After my release from prison. I have had held several jobs to include, being a personal trainer, in personal security, and a community support worker in the hospital. In the mental health arena, I have served in the capacity of director and counselor in schools, group homes and prisons. I have put on workshops and spoke at schools, churches, and various conferences. I have also continued to further my education and have received certifications in addictions, addictive behavior, and mental health.

Presently, I take any opportunity that I have, to try and help teenagers and young adults that I meet. My goal is to help them get their lives on the right track. I use my influence in assisting them in journeying in the right direction, instead of traveling into the wrong direction.

The only way to go is the RIGHT way! First, keep God first in your life. Teens, listen to your parents! Stay in school, and don't deal with any negativity that surrounds you! Don't use living in a single parent home as an excuse! Most of all, stay off the streets! There is nothing but lies and destruction in the streets!

POVERTY

You may have come from a family of poverty, but it does not mean that you must become a product of that environment. You can flip what appear to be your destiny. You can dream, rise, and soar like an eagle. There is nothing impeding you. Opportunity is here for you too! You can do anything you set your mind to do and obtain anything you desire. Just keep your mind focused on God, and channel your lifestyle on positive influences. You can achieve and accomplish the same goals, as those you may feel are more fortunate than you are! Just because someone lives in nice homes in the county or suburbs, does not mean that they are better than you are. You must change your way of thinking. It all starts in your mind! We must use our minds and cultivate our beliefs into ourt thoughts that will help us have a better way of thinking. A better way of thinking translates into a better life. We must do what is necessary to eliminate the state of impoverishment in your life. Yes, you may initially be rejected by others, while you are in poverty, but you must stand strong and keep moving forward!

Yes, I too, have been rejected. Finally, someone gave me another chance to improve and better myself. Now

I am positive, flourishing and achieving much success in my life. There is no looking back! I will never find myself in the negative situations of my past again!

As you come to him, the living stone—rejected by humans but chosen by God and precious to him – you also, like living stones, are being built into a spiritual house to be a holy priesthood, offering spiritual sacrifices acceptable to God through Jesus Christ.
I Peter 2:4-5

FIGHTING THE BATTLE

It is important to realize, as previously discussed, that it may take quite a stretch of time to build your self-image and your relationships. It is especially difficult when you are still working to restore your self-confidence and broken relationships. There are times when we tend to feel that we can't truly say that we have fully arrived! We must remember that the rebuilding process of our self-image and our relationships are opposed by the enemy, Satan. He will try to keep you bound by your past, and to make you ineffective for the Kingdom of God. The challenges of constantly trying to prove yourself to others, can be discouraging and disappointing. But we must continually equip ourselves with the sword, the Word of God! God will continue to show us areas in which growth and change is needed. He will help us overcome significant battles in our lives.

REBUILDING

Injured persons must begin to rebuild their self-image before they can effectively rebuild relationships with others. We must remember that in order to build an effective relationship, it takes two active people. The process of rebuilding can become difficult. Too often, old patterns with lack of communication, and lack of relating with others on the same level, may hinder the ability to pursue the exchange needed to start the healing process. Sometimes it becomes difficult because the offender may not be interested in rebuilding a relationship. The offended person must remember that they are accountable only for themselves. Therefore, the offended person must decide whether to give up or continue to work toward obtaining resolution.

Healing is forgiveness through the blood of Christ. It means finding comfort which repairs and restores. Forgiveness is constantly taught. Therefore, repairing and restoring must be taught as well. There must be healing of the soul and healing in our physical bodies.

Surely He has borne our grief and carried our sorrows; yet we esteemed Him stricken, Smitten by God, and afflicted. But He was wounded for our transgressions, He was bruised for our iniquities; the chastisement for our peace was upon Him, and by His strips we are healed. **Isaiah 53:4-6**

FEAR

Fear energizes us to flee when we are confronted with harm. It can overpower us! It makes any forward movement a battle that seem absurd. As fear increases, the body is prepared to shut down and curl up into a position that preserves us. We will do whatever seems reasonable to escape. Therefore, the anxiety that we feel, demands that we position ourselves in survival mode. To protect ourselves, our defense is to back away from our problem or that threatening person.

If you hate your sin enough, you will stop! Repentance means to "change, to turn around and to go the other way." You must ask yourself, "what hidden ways are you enjoying sin?" We must make every attempt to recognize our sinful performance orientation. It is not easy, because the evil practices of the flesh are stubborn.

"You must hate what is evil!"

Despair makes us dull to any advances made toward us; the possibility of arousal or any desire for intimacy is discarded. In having a repeated cycle of one's desire being discarded, their hope is shattered in disappointment, and soul deadened through despair. This leads to hatred of any desire.

We must continue to hate what is evil. We must try to avoid and resist ungodly advances made toward us. We must strive for excellence and resists the immoralities of this world.

To many, having a desire is an enemy that can be neutralized through contempt. We might fight against the arousal of any hope when someone moves toward us, offering kindness and tenderness; therefore, fear may make it look like contempt. We often feel like fools who have been set up and used by others from our past. Any hope for us, penetrates the facade of contempt, and our desire for intimacy exposes us as needy. We try to hide the feeling of shame, knowing that someone may judge us.

Listed below are statements found in two books that I had read that helped me look at things from another perspective:

In the book, **"The Cry of the Soul, How Our Emotions Reveal Our Deepest Questions about God," by Dr. Dan B. Allender and Dr. Tremper Longman III,"** it states on page 49 that, "Intimacy is a taste of reconciliation, and it is a testimony to the fact that separation and loss have been overcome." It further states, "Moments of connection reflect our hunger for redemption, for a perfect relationship with God." Although we crave redemption, we are also reluctant to let our desires exceed our control.

In the book, **"Transforming the Inner Man," by John Loren and Paula Sanford,"** it states on page 7, "Although every sinful deed was fully washed away when you accepted Jesus as your Lord, not every part of your heart was immediately able to fully appropriate the good news of that fact."

We must work on our fears as we move forward. You could be trying to move forward in your life by starting a business, an invention, a family, or a ministry. If we continue to walk in fear, it can hinder or destroy the many blessings that God has for us as we move forward into future endeavors.

God has not given us a spirit of fear, but of power, love, and a sound mind! **2 Timothy 1:7**

We must lay aside all the stresses of life to truly focus, and to clear our minds. We must not be blinded by what is happening in this world, which can hinder us from receiving what God has for us!

Wherefore seeing we also are compassed about with so great a cloud of witnesses, let us lay aside every weight, and the sin which doth so easily beset us, and let us run with patience the race that is set before us, Looking unto Jesus the author and finisher of our faith; who for the joy that was set before him endured the cross, despising the shame, and is set down at the right hand of the throne of God. **Hebrews 12:1**

SEEING GOD

Those whose hearts are purified come to understand and embrace God for who He is. We love because He first loved us.

If someone says, "I love God; and hate his brother, he is a liar; for the one who does not love his brother whom he has seen, cannot love God whom he has not seen. This commandment we have from Him, that the one who loves God should love his brother also." **I John 4:19-21.**

Sometimes the heart has been scarred or shaped by reactions from our past circumstances. Thus, we often project cruelty, and other negative factors, onto our understanding of who God is. Our minds, many declare His goodness, but our behaviors reveal what the heart really thinks.

"As a man thinks in his heart, so is he."
Proverbs 23:7

Until we can forgive those that have hurt us, and reverse the judgements we have formed against them, we will not be able to see God as He truly is. His gentleness, kindness, and loving tenderness will not be present in our lives.

Blessed are the pure in heart: for they shall see God.
Matthew 5:8

REJECTING FAULTY BELIEFS

We are all a work in progress! How do you feel about yourself? Your accomplishments? Do you really love you? Has people spoken negative things over your life that has held you captive or stuck?

We must remember that we are valuable to God! It is written in the scriptures of God's love for us. One must study the scriptures and focus on God's acceptance, favor, and love. We must learn to love ourselves! Reject any faulty beliefs you have of yourself! Reject anything anyone has spoken negatively over your life! Close your ears to anything that is not positive! Reject the *poison*! We all have fallen short and made mistakes, but learning from those mistakes, makes us a better person. You will achieve your freedom by moving forward, and not looking back.

Any false notions you have about yourself or any negative seed someone has planted over your life are really lies, planted by the enemy to keep you bound, and is meant to stop your positive progress. The Word of God is the truth! It is the *medicine* needed to sustain us. It will enable you to renew your mind! In moving forward, you may have to rid yourself of negative people, and surround yourself with people that are like minded, and are moving in a positive direction. No more stinking thinking!

"And to be renewed in the spirit of your minds, and to put on the new self, created after the likeness of God in true righteousness and holiness." **Ephesians 4:23**

I have loved you with an everlasting love; therefore, I have continued my faithfulness in you. **Jeremiah 31:3**

HELPING OTHERS

There are many ways of helping others. Helping others provide an opportunity to use something that may have been destructive in your life, to bring constructive results in someone else's life.

Expressing concern and empathizing with others provides hope. To empathize with others also brings continual healing to the one being the comforter. It is my passion, as well as a joy to see progress in someone that I have impacted. I will continue to reach the lost at any cost and give direction to anyone that needs to be guided into moving forward, in the right way!

I know that I can't reach everyone or save the world, but I believe God has certain people just for me to reach. I am willing to give back to them the wisdom and the lessons that I have learned to help them succeed. There is a call on my life to reach out to help people that are in need. I have answered my call to continue to reach the lost.

Michael W. Stanley

Blessed be God, even the Father of our Lord Jesus Christ, the Father of mercies, and the God of all comfort; Who comforteth us in all our tribulation, that we may be able to comfort them which are in any trouble, by the comfort wherewith we ourselves are comforted of God. **2 Corinthians 1:3-4**

FORGIVENESS

Forgiveness, like many other areas of our lives, doesn't happen overnight, it is a process. The length of the process will depend on the individual person, how deep the hurt, and how deep-rooted their wound is. Deeply embedded wounds will take even longer to heal.

Although the process of forgiveness may take some time, it does not mean that anyone is given a license to hold onto any anger, bitterness, or resentment! These are normal emotions during the process, but in time, these emotions can be released. Therefore, a person must work through their emotions until their final goal of forgiveness is reached.

There are many challenges in the forgiving process. I would suggest to any counselor is that they should start slowly with a victim in their healing process, and not to feel as though they will heal the victim. The victim must heal on their own, and within their own time. We must assure them that they may not forget what was done to them, but they must allow peace to enter hearts, minds, and spirit while coping with what was done to them.

I personally had to deal with forgiving others, and with

asking others to forgive me. I am not sure if all the people I wronged accepted my apologies or not. I do know that in asking them for forgiveness, it gave me relief and freedom. Forgiveness is for you, not the person that did you wrong or who has wronged you. Therefore, I had to release my hard feeling or grudges that I held against others. I don't want to miss anyone, in my mission to get it right with everyone.

First, I had to learn to forgive myself for all the evil that I had done, and for all the people that I hurt. To achieve this, I had to ask God to forgive me, and He did! One must remember that forgiveness may not be accepted by the ones that you ask to forgive you, but it releases you!

Bear with each other and forgive one another if any of you has a grievance against someone. Forgive as the Lord forgave you. **Colossians 3:13**

PLEASE FORGIVE ME!!

IN THE PAST...
I KNOW THAT I HAVE DONE A LOT OF BAD, EVIL, AND UNFORGIVING THINGS! I HAVE HURT A LOT OF PEOPLE IN THE PROCESS.

THERE ARE THINGS THAT I REMEMBER AND SOMETHINGS THAT I DON'T REMEMBER!

THEREFORE, I WOULD LIKE TO TAKE THIS OPPORTUNITY TO ASK ANYONE THAT MAY BE READING THIS BOOK. IF I HAVE HURT OR OFFENDED YOU IN ANYWAY, **PLEASE FORGIVE ME**!?

I AM SO SORRY FOR ANY HURT OR ANGUISH THAT I MAY HAVE CAUSED YOU, AND I AM ASKING THAT, YOU FIND IT IN YOUR HEART, TO **PLEASE FORGIVE ME**!

ALTHOUGH I AM A WORK IN PROGRESS, GOD IS NOT FINISHED WITH ME YET! I AM NOT THE MAN THAT I USE TO BE!

PLEASE EXCEPT THE **NEW** ME!

MY RECENT ENCOUNTER WITH GOD

It took me months, after I made the announcement about writing a book, to finish this book. I now understand that the reason for the delay was because God was working on me. I couldn't complete the process until God completed the process in me. My encounter with the moving of God upon my life recently happened. It was part of the plan God had for me. The experience and transformation had to be fulfilled, to ensure that it was included in this book!

I got renewed and filled by God's Holy Spirit in a church conference in Charlotte, NC. The Holy Spirit was truly in the room! It was moving from the first day of the conference, starting with the Meet and Greet portion of the service. We went around the room and introduced ourselves. Some guests gave some personal testimonies about how God changed their lives. I was amazed, to hear that several people there spoke about being incarcerated and sentenced to life with no parole. That was also my plight when I was sentenced. Another person testified that she had been addicted to cocaine, and God delivered her too! Not to mention, they are now living successful lives! Their testimonies were something that I could fully identify with. I finally decided to introduce myself and tell them a little bit about my past, and about my current projects. The Meet and Greet didn't last very long, but it could have, because so many of us had so much to share, but not enough time that evening. We all had to get dinner, and all the restaurants were very crowded. It was so crowded that we all had to split up and eat in different places. We were also conscious of time and wanted to get a good night sleep to be ready for the service the following day.

The next day, while entering the room for service. I felt a flow of peace and love that filled the room. This love and peace appeared to have been felt by everyone there. You can sometimes relate to feeling this way with one or maybe two persons, but the whole room of people is inconceivable. Wow! Everyone interacted with each other, embracing, and encouraging one another, as we went from table to table. Several of us had vendor tables with our business products displayed. I was included in the number and sold my products during the conference as well. Everyone supported each other and bought from one another. There was one person that didn't purchase anything from my table, but came over, and shook my hand, and gave me a donation toward my foundation. That was only the beginning of that day.

The guest speaker was a powerful woman of God, who spoke over my life! I never met this woman of God before, but she read me from top to bottom! She talked about all the things that I had been through and the things that I had seen in my past. I am not trying to tell all my business, but she said that, I had been overlooked by many, and that I was like Joseph in the Bible. She also stated that I was once in the pit, and then to prison! Wow! She even called out all the current projects that I have been working on, like this book! Prior to her prophesying to me, I had been sitting at my table, and I had written down something that was on my heart, on a note pad, and she even mentioned that! God was really speaking through her about me! She encouraged my soul, and it enlighten me. This whole experience increased my faith because I knew this had to be God!

God has always spoken to me. He has given me the many gifts, but I do have a strong gift in discernment. I can see the wrong spirits on people, and I can see when people are being phony and have the wrong motives. I must admit that I must learn how to control my candidness, because when I see the wrong type of spirit, I usually call it out! Therefore, sometimes I share it with someone that is close to me, and sometimes it can be at the wrong time.

Before this service ended, I received the gift of the Holy Spirit. I was anointed to continue to walk in my calling (that I accept), and I was Baptized! I also received other prophesies (a word from God), through the host of the conference, and her husband! Therefore, I was used several times during the conference, and I loved every bit of it! I can truly say that my life has not been the same! That experience has equipped me for the things to come as, I continue to move forward in my life.

GROWING AND MOVING FORWARD

A mature adult knows better, "a healthy respect for reality" they know for the most part, if they do good, good things will happen. If they do nothing, nothing will happen. If they do bad, bad things will happen. To have dual respect for positive and negative sides of reality is referred to as "wisdom." I lacked wisdom, responsibility, and discipline in my life. I allowed the *poison* in my mind to steer me in the wrong direction. I made some terrible choices in life, and I have paid some very harsh and tough consequences for my wrong actions.

It is not by accident that my life was spared from the streets. My current goals are to impart wisdom into the minds of our youth; to inspire men so that they can recover from losses they experienced in life, which was due bad choices. There is victory in recovery. Recovery is the *medicine* used to change your way of thinking from a negative, to a positive behavior. Direct your thoughts and actions, toward having a relationship with God, to include a consistent prayer life. Include all the things, coupled with positive influences, and it will help you through the process of moving forward into society. One must face the obstacles of life, with an orientation toward growth. This growth process includes the development of abilities, gaining knowledge, and facing the negative attributes about oneself, that may need changing.

I dranked the *poison* of life and still lived!! Praise God! What I went through was very traumatic! To get over the trauma, you must go back to the event that caused you the trauma!

The Bible is very clear that, it is those who diligently seek Him who receive a response from Him. **Hebrews 11:6**

I recommend beginning where you are. If you decide that your desire to change isn't powerful enough, admit to yourself that your desire isn't enough. Ask God to help you and give, Him the desire that you are lacking. You know that it is God's work within us that gives us the desire to do His will, so ask Him for what you desire.

In my atmosphere of hunger, dependency, and the willingness to seek God, God imparted His holiness to me. He revealed His perfect will and entrusted me the power to overcome the evil that put me in prison in the first place. I then became an effective channel of His blessing for others. I directed others who were weak or in the process of giving up on life and showed them the way, while on their journey to recovery.

Don't allow your feelings and emotions to dictate your reality. Instead, listen to God who promised that:

"Never will I leave you, never will I forsake you." **Hebrews 3:5**

You must determine, who you can reveal your true self to, so that God's full healing power will be able to operate in your life. Then you can begin the incredible journey of restoration. When you connect with the right people, doors will open, and what you believe, and speak out of your mouth, you can make happen.

God has communicated to me the love and the affirmation I had always longed for from my earthly father, (whom I never knew!), Yes! God was the *medicine* that I needed in my mind, heart, and soul! Sometimes you must go through complete hell to reach Heaven!

Restoration – When considering the restoration of past offenders, we are constantly confronted by those who doubt that past offenders can ever change.

In some cases, we must allow somethings to die in our lives so that God can change us. I stop drinking the **poison** *of life and started taking the* **medicine** *that changed and restored my life!*

THINGS TO PONDER

Children who grow up with dysfunctional parents or who live in other harmful environments will eventually growto recent their take on life. Many of them will blame God, and for whatever reason, they may see God as unfair and uncaring, even if their parent(s) try to influence them otherwise.

Parents become frustrated and there is no peace because they struggle over certain behaviors from their children. Misbehaviors will change only if the child changes. Usually, something drastic must happen to them for them to understand what their parents are trying to teach them. It can be a traumatic experience, like seeing a close friend or family member, shot, and killed, or even die in their arms. A disturbing painful situation had to occur to make them change. This is something that I pray will not happen to them, and that I am allowed to share using my own experiences that I learned from the street. My hope is that my influence and my personal account of things that I have gone through, will help them before any traumatic experiences take place in their lives.

Sometimes, deep inside a child's mind, (perhaps unknown even to himself), he will nurse a deep strong hold of anger towards someone he loved or trusted, and even God. Because of that stronghold in the child's mind, he will draw on his sinful lifestyle to justify his wrongdoing and will be unable to draw close to God.

Well... I am here to tell you, if you have adopted a negative self-image, God wants to correct this error by speaking your identity into your spirit through His word. He also uses the words of other believers, who He sends to communicate truth to you; He will give you direct revelation to your soul during times of intimacy with Him. I choose to believe in the new reality instead of the old identity!

The enemy will try to keep you in bondage. Even after God changes you, he will lie to you, to cause you to believe that the old guy (you of the past) still exists. You must choose to believe God instead of the lie, and accept by faith, your new identity in Christ. The "new identity" is an identity that reflects objective truth in your present reality, rather than the projections of society. Additionally, it does not include misguided authority figures, or the destructive environment that was once a part of your past. The perception of our identity is initially acquired through our life's experiences. We are influenced by the opinion of others and by the Word of God. We must eventually decide whose opinion we are going to accept as valid and true – man's opinion or God's.

If we accept God's view of us, He will engrave it in our hearts. The process needed to uncover our old perception of ourselves, and to accept the new view of ourselves. God has made a way of escape, for that child, young man, young woman, who decides that he or she is no longer going to follow in the sinful ways of the streets or destructive lifestyle. The way of escape is to turn to God to be set free! I am a living testimony!

Events can be life-changing, and yet we all must keep living after that defining moment. That means, looking to God, who is our source and strength, to make the right decisions every day. It takes time, but you must keep working at becoming who God wants you to become!

But if the wicked will turn from all his sins that he hath committed, and keep all my statutes, and do that which is lawful and right, he shall surely live, he shall not die. All his transgressions that he hath committed, they shall not be mentioned unto him: in his righteousness that he hath done he shall live. ***Ezekiel 18:21-22***

ABOUT THIS BOOK

You must determine who you can reveal your true self to your struggles, and issues of life, and the fears that you face. You may decide to seek help from a Counselor, Therapist, Pastor, Mentor or Friend. The person you choose, must have your best interest at heart. They must be willing and able to see you through the challenges that you may face during your healing process. You must be mentally prepared, so that God's full healing power will be able to operate. You will then be ready to begin the incredible journey of restoration.

My book is designed to tell my story. Hopefully, my story will prevent, someone who feels that they have no other choice, but to be a by-product of their environment. Yes, you have a choice to be all that you can be in life and to do better in life, despite any bad choices you have made in your past. If bad choices have *poisoned* your mind or have allowed you to be incarcerated, you can make yourself better while being incarcerated. I encourage you to choose a life of hope and great expectation. Continue or get an education and become an agent of change in any environment!

Some of you may be saying to yourselves. "What if I

don't even have the desire or will to enter into a relationship with God?" If you want a change in your life, the answer is simple. Ask Him to give you what is missing. Your will and desire if you are transparent (honest) with God. God will always meet you where you are and take you where you need to be! He is a gracious and a wonderful God! Therefore, ask and keep asking, God to help you.

"God rewards those who earnestly seek Him." **Hebrews 11:6**

If God can do it for me! He can do it for you! I am an Agent of Change!

God still has a lot for me to do, for such a time as this. My passion is to see others delivered and set free, from the awful and destructive lifestyles of the streets. God has given me my beauty for ashes, the oil of joy and the garment of praise! He rescued, delivered, and restored me! Only God could have done this for me! I am not a perfect person. God is still making and molding me. Even today, I still work on building better relationships with first my family, and my friends.

What I went through, happened! Who I **_was_** existed! I needed my mistakes to help me learn and grow. I look back on my misbehaviors and mistakes, not to look back on my past, but to continue to move forward and get me to where God wants me to go. Because of God, I am now, headed to the TOP!

The Spirit of the Lord God is upon me; because the Lord hath anointed me to preach good tidings unto the meek; he hath sent me to bind up the brokenhearted, to proclaim liberty to the captives, and the opening of the prison to them that are bound; To proclaim the acceptable year of the Lord, and the day of vengeance of our God; to comfort all that mourn; To appoint unto them in Zion, to give unto them beauty for ashes, the oil of joy for mourning, the garment of praise for the spirit of heaviness; that they might be called trees of righteousness, the planting of the Lord, that he might be glorified. **Isaiah 61:1-3**

ABOUT THE AUTHOR

Mr. Michael W. Stanley BS, CAC-AD

Michael W. Stanley

Michael W. Stanley is a native Washingtonian.

Mr. Stanley was raised by a single parent and is the middle child of five boys. Michael attended and graduated from the District of Columbia Public schools. He later furthered his education and graduated Cum Laude at Coppin State University in Baltimore, MD, with a B.S. degree in Applied Psychology. He is a life coach, counselor, motivational speaker, mentor, an avid reader, and a sports and body building enthusiast.

Being a product of inner-city life and all that it entails, Michael fell prey to the fast-paced destructive lifestyle that continues to fascinate many of our youth today. His choices and actions led him down a path to incarceration.

Michael used this time of trouble to reflect, and build a relationship with God, which allowed him to be free, renewed and transformed. Reflection allowed him to look beyond himself, and to God, and to being a guiding light to others. His hope is to instill in others the idea of not, repeating bad choices and actions, and traveling down the road to destruction, while journeying through life.

Michael knows first-hand about the pipeline to prison and the vicious cycles that continues to haunt the minds of our children that the *lies* of the street create.

Michael did not let his past circumstances deter, who he was to become. He has become a voice for change!

Michael W. Stanley

Michael, who is also a certified drug addiction and behavior tac counselor, has over 25 years of counseling and crisis intervention experience, and has held many professional positions in the health care field. Michael was also instrumental in starting the first counseling center in the Penitentiary. He also served as Director of several group homes in the inner city of Baltimore, MD. Michael currently speaks as "A Voice of Experience" today in many youth centers, workshops, seminars, and colleges. He is also, an active voice of transparency, as he continues to visit the inner city-streets today.

Michael is the Founder/President of "I Make Positive Attempts to Change Teens," (I.M.P.A.C.T.) Foundation Inc. The I.M.P.A.C.T. Foundation is the vessel to help troubled and struggling inner city youth. Michael's vision and desire is to be part of the solution, "*If I can help them change the way they think, I can help them make better decisions*." Michael has been where they are and where they could possibly be headed, in the wrong direction!

I.M.P.A.C.T., means "I MAKE POSITIVE ATTEMPTS TO CHANGE TEENS" through his foundation, Michael is hopeful that true transformation to productive citizenship will occur.

Through customized groups, and one-on-one counseling sessions, seminars, and workshops, "I MAKE POSITIVE ATTEMPTS TO CHANGE TEENS," (I.M.P.A.C.T.) Foundations Inc. is committed to helping at risk-teens and young adults feel better about themselves and make better decisions. This is accomplished through encouragement; assistance in seeking and elevating higher levels of education, and in motivation, to strive for greater accomplishments than their environment may suggest they can achieve.

Michael has also newly founded another foundation, called, "Creating Responsible Youth" (CRY). Michael's desire is for youth to follow their dreams. Hopefully, his influences, encouragement, and engaging workshops, can lead youth into furthering their education. This will equip them to be responsible adults, in the workplace, and their overall life's journey.

IN MEMORY OF MY DEAR NEPHEW

Garry L. Stanley Sr.
February 12, 1977 – October 2, 2021

Bibliography

Boundaries with Kids, When to say YES, when to say No, to Help Your Children Gain Control of Their Lives, byDr. Henry Cloud and Dr. John Townsend, Zondervan Publishing House, Grand Rapids, MI

49530, 1998
The Future Is Now, Children are Not Born with Boundaries, Part 1, page 18

Science in Action, Careers in Psychology, see Haney C., "Mental health issues in long-term solitary and 'supermax' confinement." Crime and Delinquency, 49 (1), 124-156, 2014, Retrieved from http://www.supermaxed.com/NewSupermaxMaterials/ Haney-Mental Healthissues.pd

Pains of Imprisonment, Wiley Online Library, http://onlinelibrary.wiley.com, Sykes (1958/20007)

To My Dear Brothers
Who I Love Dearly

Anthony, Garry, Kenneth, John